AMERICA IN CONTEXT

AMERICA IN CONTEXT

A PURSUIT OF THE EXEMPLARY

BOB DOWELL

ISBN: 9798877530867

ACKNOWLEDGEMENTS

A special *thank you* to Lori H and TMBG
for your helpful suggestions.

Calling All Patriots

Patriots provide the pillars for sustaining an exemplary democracy
Their continuous extolling of its virtues is an absolute necessity!
How else are its youth and immigrants expected to perceive
If seasoned patriots forget their patron responsibility?

How else its youth and immigrants to perceive America's context whole
And thereby know its foundational vision that sustains its exemplary role?
Only in knowing can they experience love, loyalty, and devotion to that role,
Only in hearing its foundational vision——its "city upon a hill" story——well told.

Introduction to America in Context[1]: A Pursuit of the Exemplary

Question Asked:

"Bob, can you verify that *pursuit of the exemplary* has been a major factor in America's context?"

My Response:

Yes. If you will join me in a historical tour of America's context, you will see that *pursuit of the exemplary* has been a major factor therein.

Present State of The Pursuit:

Sadly, however, America is presently[2] experiencing a time of confusion, a time when its foundational vision—"a city upon a hill"—appears to be largely forgotten or ignored. Self-aggrandizement and political partisanship too

---

[1]   *context*, meaning the setting in which something exists.

[2]   *presently:* 2023, the year of this writing

often take precedence over the good of the country. Patriotism and common sense seem amiss nationwide.

Witnessing such confusion, I think, "Where are those wise and judicious leaders like John Winthrop, Thomas Jefferson, Elizabeth Cady Stanton, Abraham Lincoln, Martin Luther King Jr., who, in the past, positively stirred minds and hearts, nudging the nation forward in its 'city upon a hill' vision—meaning a vision to pursue the exemplary—meaning to move forward seeking to become the best a nation can be?"

Result Hoped For:

It is hoped that a guided tour viewing and assessing historical highlights of America's context that reveal defining insights concerning its pursuit of the exemplary—from its beginning to its present stalemate—might help dispel confusion and provide enlightenment and motivation for resuming that pursuit. So, dear reader, I invite you to join me—with open mind and measured judgment—in a tour of America's context that reveals, undeniably, historical evidence of America's pursuit of the exemplary.

The following TOUR CONTENTS map the historical route of our tour.

TOUR CONTENTS:
THE STOP, THE TIME, THE
NUDGER[3], THE EVENT

---

[3]   I am introducing a new word—*nudger*— meaning the leader of any major action
or event that nudges America forward in pursuit of the exemplary.

LET THE TOUR BEGIN

GREETINGS AND WELCOME TO THE TOUR!

My name is Bob Dowell, and I will be your guide for this historical tour. It is an honor and a privilege to be your guide. You might also like to know that I am a retired professor, an avid patriot, and that I have recently completed extensive research on America's context. Consequently, I hope to be able to pass on to you the most relevant portions of that context relating to our topic—America's pursuit of the exemplary—and to do so in such a way that the message will be both enjoyable and informative. Knowing that the effectiveness of a message depends heavily on its delivery medium, I have chosen the travelogue, outlined above, as the medium for delivering this message. I want to diminish the historical distance between you, dear reader, and the event so that you feel you are there actually witnessing great leaders judiciously, through word and deed, nudging the nation forward in its pursuit of the exemplary.

To aid in analyzing and understanding the historical events that comprise this tour, I will provide you—previous to each stop—relevant information defining the context of the event.

Please listen carefully as I relate information defining the historical context of our first stop.

FIRST STOP

Time: 1630

Nudger: John Winthrop, governor of the Massachusetts Bay Colony

Event: His sermon entitled "A Model of Christian Charity"

Context:

America's history may be thought of as a pursuit of the exemplary. Why so? Think of the undeniable connection between America and the Reformation. Think of the Reformation as having birthed America via the Puritans. Why so? Think of two of America's three earliest permanent settlements—the Plymouth Colony of 1620 and the Massachusetts Bay Colony of 1630. Both colonies were led by Puritans, who left England hoping to achieve in America, the New World, what, despite intensive effort, they could not achieve in Old World England. Many Puritans came to view America in a providential light, viewing this New World wilderness as the divinely designated place to pursue the exemplary for both church and community. Thus, their vision of a Bible-based commonwealth, "a city upon a hill" for all the world to see, and hopefully emulate. The "city upon a hill" phrase is a biblical allusion. See Matthew 5:14–16.[4] Though the Reformation's call to purify the church took hold early on in the Church of England, the reform did not reach the level thought necessary by a large number of its members—those referred to as Puritans—who adamantly insisted that purifying the church meant making it like the New Testament church, and that it must happen if God's redemption covenant was to work.

Thus, it becomes clear that the Puritans were definitely birthed by the Reformation—the movement to purify the church initiated by Martin Luther's Ninety-five Theses written and posted in 1517. England responded early on to the Reformation by passing in 1534 the Act of Supremacy, declaring their king rather than the pope as supreme head of the church there. This act, however, was not enough to satisfy a large number of believers, who insisted that reform must continue until the church became like the New Testament church. As a result of their unrelenting insistence, they were called Puritans, an intended derogatory term. Yet despite increasingly hostile resistance, they held firmly to their stance.

They viewed the New Testament as God's ultimate plan for the redemption of humanity, and the church as the means of witnessing

---

[4]   *In the Sermon on the Mount, Jesus, speaking to his disciples, says, "You are the light of the world." Then he adds that "a city built upon a hill cannot be hidden" and that "a lamp is placed upon a stand so it gives light to everyone in the house." Thus he says, "In the same way, let your light shine before others that they may see your good works and glorify your Father in heaven."

that plan to the world. Consequently, they reasoned, it is imperative that the church stay on course, meaning to carefully follow the script—scripture—as exemplified by the New Testament church. The Reformation was a call to purify the church, a call largely due to the evolving practice of allotting *church tradition* equal authority to that of scripture, thereby instituting questionable practices such as the selling of indulgences— reducing the amount of time a person might spend in Purgatory. In England, the Puritans held fast to their purification doctrine. Their thinking may be summed up as follows.

Viewing the Old Testament, they read in Genesis chapters two and three the story of Adam and Eve and the Fall. The story interpreted: "In Adam's fall/We sinned all,"[5] thereby leaving humanity thenceforth doomed. Only by God's grace could humanity be redeemed. Further reviewing of Genesis revealed that God in his mercy initiates a redemption plan—Noah and the flood. Sadly, however, Noah's post-flood unrighteousness unravels that plan. Yet God, in His mercy, initiates another plan, the covenant plan revealed in Genesis 12:1–3. Abraham—a man of faultless faith— and his descendants, the Israelites, become God's chosen people to facilitate the plan.

They noted that the remainder of the Old Testament after Genesis 12:1–3 primarily addresses the development of this

---

[5] *The couplet, "In Adam's fall/We sinned all," comes from the *New England Primer, the* popular reading primer of the colonies, first designed and published around 1690. The *Primer* utilized religious content to teach reading skills. Lessons on sin, death, and salvation were addressed through alphabetic rhymed couplets, prayers, and scripture. The couplet that we have just referenced—"In Adam's fall/We sinned all"—is the rhyming couplet for the letter *A*. (See page 28 in *The New England Primer, edited by R. A. Sheats, published by Psalm 78 Ministries, 2018.*)

covenant redemption plan—the story of Abraham and his descendants, the Israelites, God's chosen people—to witness His redemption plan to all the world. The story stretches over hundreds of years, but ultimately the Israelites' lack of faith and obedience brings an end to the Old Testament redemption plan, now referred to as the *old covenant*.

Happily, though, as prophesied by Old Testament prophet Jeremiah (31:31–34), God initiates a new covenant, the subject of the New Testament. Not only does God initiate a new covenant, he so loved the world, he sent his son Jesus Christ to shape and exemplify the new covenant and to found the church, a body of believers to witness the new covenant plan throughout all the world. His earthly mission finished—ministry, cross, and resurrection—Christ returns to heaven to await the church's fulfilment of its mission. The Puritans noted that the church's mission went remarkably well in its early New Testament years, but, as history confirms, eventually impurities threatened to destroy it. In 1517, Martin Luther—priest, theologian, professor—posted on the church door in Wittenberg, Germany, his Ninety-five Theses questioning church purity—an act that triggered the Reformation. The Reformation, in turn, birthed the Puritans, many of whom, after years of harassment in their dedication to church purification in the Old World—Reformation or no—began to entertain the vision of doing so in New World America, where they would be virtually free of oppressive interference from both clerical and civil authorities. In fact, many Puritans began to view themselves as the new covenanted Israelites to get the church back on track and save God's redemptive plan.

They reasoned thus: *Had not the Israelites failed to carry out God's redemptive plan, and was not the church—Reformation or no—now, like the Israelites of old, failing to carry out God's new redemptive plan? And did not God promise that all families would be blessed through the faith of Abraham? And did not Abraham believe God, and did not God credit it to him as righteousness?*[6] *Thus, reasoned the Puritans, may not God now be calling us to go where he directs us to go, to do what he directs us to do that his redemptive plan may be pursued as intended and witnessed in its purity?*

And in this frame of mind, many Puritans began to envision themselves as God's newly chosen Israelites to establish in the New World wilderness of America a Bible-based commonwealth. Let's note this vision as revealed in the following excerpts from four documents included in *Heritage of American Literature: Beginnings to the Civil War*.

Edward Johnson, in his epic *Wonder-Working Providence of Scion's Savior in New England (1654)* writes, "When England began to decline in religion…Christ, the glorious king of His churches, raises an army out of our English nation for freeing His people… Christ creates a new England to muster up the first of His forces."[7]

In William Bradford's *Of Plymouth Plantation* (1630–1650), we note that Bradford viewed the colony's history as a providential happening.[8]

Cotton Matter's epic *Magnalia Christi Americana* (1702) begins, "I write of the wonders of the Christian religion, flying from the

---

[6] See Genesis 12:1–3; 15:6.

[7] James E. Miller Jr., ed. *Heritage of American Literature: Beginnings to the Civil War* (Harcourt, Brace, Jovanovich, 1991), 109–110.

[8] Miller, *Heritage of American Literature*, 59, 69.

depravations of Europe to the American strand, and assisted by the holy Author of that religion."[9]

Although this providential view is voiced in various Puritan writings, nowhere is it more clearly and instructively expressed than in John Winthrop's sermon, "A Model of Christian Charity," delivered in 1630 to the Massachusetts Bay colonists on their way to America. Winthrop explains that, by providence, humanity is diverse—rich and poor, weak and strong, eminent and lowly—but ideally bonded through Christian love, the bond of perfection, the bond to be cultivated and perpetuated by the Bay Colony. He further explains that this bond must be grounded in a covenant relationship between the colonists and God and that its success depends on the colonists' obedience to the covenant. No doubt, Winthrop is thinking how Israelite disobedience wrecked the *old covenant* and how, as the Reformation confirmed, the new covenant was being wrecked by the church's increasing disregard of its commission as scripturally directed and obediently followed by the early New Testament church. Thus, for the Bay Colony to be the *new Israelites*, that is to say the new covenanted people, they must be obedient to their perceived covenant with God. They must exemplify their belief that God had commissioned them to establish a Bible-based commonwealth in the New World and thereby become a light to the world, "a city upon a hill." Their safe journey over a perilous sea and a safe landing was viewed as God's ratification of their mission. Consequently, it was imperative they live up to their exemplary promise. To do otherwise would make them a grossly disobedient and perjured people in God's sight. In Winthrop's own words, "Thus

---

[9]   Miller, *Heritage of American Literature,* 321.

stands the cause between God and us…We have taken out a commission, the Lord hath given us leave to draw our own articles… Now, if the Lord shall please to hear us, and bring us in peace to the place we desire, then he hath ratified this covenant and sealed our commission…but if we shall neglect the observation of these articles which are the ends we have propounded…the Lord will surely break out in wrath against us, be revenged of such a perjured people." For maintaining obedience to their covenant, he exhorts the colonists to follow the counsel of the prophet Micah, "to do justly, to love mercy, and to walk humbly with your God" (Micah 6:8).[10]

TOUR GUIDE REFLECTS ON THE FIRST STOP

Note that the goal of the Reformation was to purify the church. To the Puritans that meant making it like the New Testament church—each Christian congregation the conscience of its local community and their composite the conscience of the commonwealth. Is that not Winthrop's message in his sermon, "A Model of Christian Charity," a reminder to the colonists that Christian love is the essential bond for perfecting a commonwealth and that the success of their New World mission depends upon their practice thereof—living their "city upon a hill" vision?

Sidebar

I wish to pose a few questions for you to keep in mind as we continue our tour. As we all know, church and state in America are

---

[10] Miller, *Heritage of American Literature*, 97–98.

separate, yet in our democracy, is the church not free to pursue its mission, free to witness Christianity hoping hearers may believe and follow in the footsteps of its founder and exemplar, Jesus Christ, thereby exemplifying and promoting love, peace, and goodwill? What could be more exemplary? What could be more beneficial to a nation? Would that nation not be "a city upon a hill"? And would that city not be like the city Jesus commanded to his disciples in his Sermon on the Mount? "You are the light of the world. A city that is built on a hill cannot be hidden" (Matthew 5:14). And is not the son of God speaking for the father who sent him? Consequently, what could be more exemplary than pursuing the will of God?

Let the Tour Continue

Now, please listen carefully as I relate relevant information defining the historical context of the second stop.

SECOND STOP

Time: 1776

Nudger: Thomas Jefferson

Event: the Declaration of Independence

Context:

As we continue our tour, let us keep in mind the exemplary vision for America shared by two of its earliest colonies: the vision as notably voiced by John Winthrop, governor of the Massachusetts Bay Colony, in his sermon, "A Model of Christian Charity" (1630), and the vision beginning to be implemented in America as notably related by William Bradford, governor of the Plymouth Colony, in his history, *Of Plymouth Plantation* (1620–1647).[11] Thus, we move from a sermon defining the two colonies'

---

[11] See Miller, *Heritage of American Literature*, 93–98 (for Winthrop) and 50–84 (for Bradford).

vision of the exemplary to a history noting special acts of providence ratifying the vision. With this in mind, we fast-forward almost a century and a half to 1776, at which time there are thirteen colonies that have formed the Continental Congress to represent them in their quarrel with England.

Unable to persuade their mother country to grant the governing freedom they believe due them, they publicity declare their independence, their justification for doing so, and publish it in a document entitled the Declaration of Independence. The Continental Congress first appointed a committee of five to draft the declaration. Though the committee included such notable writers as John Adams and Benjamin Franklin, they deferred to Thomas Jefferson, Adams reportedly saying, "You can write ten times better than I can." Whatever the case, Jefferson drafted the Declaration, and the Continental Congress, after minimal revision, approved it.

The document reveals that the reformational spirit advocating the pursuit of the exemplary was prevalent throughout America's colonies. As previously noted, two of America's earliest colonies—the Plymouth Colony (1620) and the Massachusetts Bay Colony (1630)—chose to settle in America to form an exemplary commonwealth, providentially sanctioned. In 1776, all thirteen colonies, in their Declaration of Independence,[12] voice their ratification of the exemplary "city upon a hill" vision. In this foundational document, they declare "that the laws of nature and nature's God" entitle them to separate from England and become a separate nation. Next, they not only express their cause for doing so but also their vision, their

---

[12] To view the Declaration of Independence, see Miller, *Heritage of American Literature*, 590–594.

creed to guide them in forming an exemplary new nation. "We hold these truths to be self-evident: that all men are created equal; that they are endowed by their Creator with certain inalienable rights; that among these are life, liberty, and the pursuit of happiness." Martin Luther King, Jr., in his famous "I Have a Dream" speech, refers to this expression as America's creed, and rightfully so. Our word *creed* originates from the Latin word *credo*, meaning "I believe." And does not this expression from our Declaration of Independence express a belief that defines and justifies the exemplary? And does this exemplary creed not justify the need to form a new nation as well as define a blueprint for its formation?

The expression might very well remind one of the Apostles' Creed recited in the worship services of many churches confirming their belief in Jesus Christ. This is not to imply that the members of the Continental Congress were Christ's disciples, but ascribing the equality creed—inalienable equal rights gifted all men—to the laws of nature and the God of nature surely indicates they definitely believed in God. Another strong indicator of their belief in God is the imagery engraved on the Great Seal. After approving the declaration, they commissioned a design for the Great Seal for the new nation. On its reverse side is the eye of providence positioned above an unfinished pyramid of thirteen layers and capped by the Latin phrase *annuit coeptis*. The Latin phrase is a motto explaining the symbolism of the eye image. Translated, it means, "He [God] favors our undertakings," and *undertakings* means the thirteen colonies that became the thirteen states of the United States of America, represented by the thirteen layers of the unfinished pyramid, symbolically a new nation represented by the ancient symbol of strength and permanence, the pyramid. Furthermore, the eye of providence above the pyramid symbolizes divine approval and guidance of the new nation. Although the Great Seal's design was not completed and approved until 1782, it was commissioned in 1776 by the Continental Congress following its approval of the Declaration of Independence. You may have noticed, engraved on the back of our dollar bill, both the obverse and reverse (front and back) of the Great Seal, and between the dual images, the words "In God We Trust." More later about the Great Seal inscribed on the dollar bill.

TOUR GUIDE REFLECTS ON THE SECOND STOP

We have now witnessed the colonies' vision of becoming a nation, not just another nation, not just another commonwealth, but, like the early Plymouth and Massachusetts Bay Colonies, a vision of becoming an exemplary commonwealth, a God-sanctioned exemplary commonwealth, a city upon a hill, a beacon light to the world. Does its published creed—"We hold these truths to be self-evident"—not state such? It certainly does, but the crucial question is the following: does the new nation implement its creed? Or, phrased differently, does it live its creed? That's the heart of the matter. But before we begin condemning, let us keep in mind that, at this point, their independence is declared but is yet to be won. And the independence has to be won in order to pursue the exemplary embodied in their stated creed. Another important factor to recognize: it is unfair and unjust to judge a past historical situation solely by contemporary standards. To be fair and just, an action or attitude must be viewed in the context of its time frame. For example, it would be patently unfair and unjust to condemn Thomas Jefferson because he owned slaves and ignore the fact that he was thoroughly opposed to slavery, calling it a "moral depravity" and a "hideous blot." He recognized it as a threat to the nation's unity and sought ways to abolish it. Though it became one of the deletions in the revision for passage, Jefferson included in an early draft of the Declaration of Independence a section condemning slavery.

Thus, we must note that Jefferson, though a slave owner, personally opposed slavery, as did many other slave owners whose conscience was troubled by the immorality of slavery, but most remained silent, realizing the adverse consequences of abolition without a national amnesty program preparing slaves for freedom and compensating slave owners for their financial loss. Yet all did not remain silent—Jefferson, a prime example—and in time moral conscience won out, as we will observe at our next stop. Jefferson called slavery a "moral depravity," presumably considering it a violation of the law of nature and nature's God ("all men are created equal"). He feared it as a great threat to the survival of the new nation, but thought its successful abolition depended on a democratic process in which slave owners consented to free their slaves in a wide-scale emancipation act. The issue became more and more heated as abolitionists pushed harder and harder for abolishing slavery. Finally, the issue divided the states into the North and the South, the North—the Union—opposing slavery, and the South—the Confederacy—defending slavery. The Civil War began in April of 1861 when Confederate soldiers fired on Union-held Fort Sumter and effectively ended at the battle of Appomattox in April of 1865, the Union winning, but with years of contentious civil rights issues to follow. Our tour will elaborate on Abraham Lincoln's judicious leadership in America's pursuit of the exemplary during the Civil War years of the nineteenth century and the judicious leadership of Martin Luther King Jr. in America's pursuit of the exemplary in the twentieth century.

We shall return to the slavery issue in our fourth stop—the historical 1863 stop—but first, let's address another civil rights issue affecting more or less half the nation's citizens: women's civil rights, the other large group not included in the equality creed. So please listen carefully as I relate relevant information defining the historical context of our third stop.

THIRD STOP

Time: 1848
Nudger: Elizabeth Cady Stanton
Event: the Declaration of Sentiments

Context:

Undeniably, the two major leaders of the women's rights movement in the nineteenth century were Elizabeth Cady Stanton and Susan B. Anthony. However, it was Elizabeth Cady Stanton who first organized a women's rights convention in America. She was born into a politically active family. Her father was an attorney who served in Congress; her mother participated in his campaigns. Elizabeth, in turn, married a politically active attorney, Henry B. Stanton. Both being active abolitionists, they went to England on their honeymoon in order to attend a world antislavery convention in London. Upon arrival, she learned, much to her chagrin, that women were barred as delegates. No doubt this incident was neither to be forgotten nor passively accepted by her.

Eight years later, she had succeeded in organizing a women's rights convention to be held in Seneca Falls, New York. Not only did she organize the convention, but she also drafted its Declaration of Sentiments.[13] Ingeniously, she took Jefferson's masterfully written Declaration of Independence and converted it into the Declaration of Sentiments by making certain key revisions, such as revising Jefferson's "all men are created equal" to read "all men *and women* are created equal." Where Jefferson uses a repetitive list of grievances all beginning with "He has" to condemn King George, Stanton utilizes the same effective device. Whereas Jefferson uses "He has" referring to King George, Stanton uses "He has" referring to "mankind," thereby directing her grievances against *men*. Stanton also utilizes Jefferson's preface to the "He has" grievances against King George. Jefferson writes, "The history of the present king of Great Britain is a history of repeated injuries and usurpations…To prove this, let facts be presented to a candid world." Following this preface is a preponderance of charges, each beginning with the phrase "He has." Stanton writes, "The history of mankind is a history of injuries and usurpations on the part of *man* toward women, having in direct object the establishment of an absolute tyranny over her. To prove this let facts be presented to a candid world." Following this preface is a preponderance of charges, each beginning with "He has."

Keeping in mind that the time frame is 1848, let us note several of the "He has" charges that Stanton makes against mankind:

---

[13] See Miller, *Heritage of American Literature*, 1835–1838.

"He has never permitted her to exercise her inalienable right to the elective franchise."

"He has compelled her to submit to laws, in the formation of which she had no voice."

"He has made her, if married, in the eye of the law, civilly dead."

"He has taken from her all right in property, even to the wages she earns."

"He has denied her the facilities for obtaining a thorough education—all colleges being closed against her."

"He has endeavored, in every way that he could to destroy her confidence in her own powers, to lessen her self-respect, and to make her willing to lead a dependent and abject life."

TOUR GUIDE REFLECTS ON STOP THREE

As Luther's Ninety-five Theses triggered the Reformation in Europe, so Stanton's Seneca Falls Convention triggered the women's rights movement in America. Though Stanton did not live to savor it, seventy-two years later, the passing of the Nineteenth

Amendment to the Constitution (1920) gave women the right to vote. Unquestionably, Stanton deserves to be recognized as the one who initiated the momentum that eventually effected its passage. Does she not then deserve to be recognized as one of America's wise and judicious leaders who stirred minds and hearts, thereby nudging America forward in its pursuit of the exemplary? Surely so!

LET THE TOUR CONTINUE

Please listen carefully as I relate relevant information defining the historical context of our fourth stop.

Time: 1863

Nudger: Abraham Lincoln

Event: the Emancipation Proclamation and the Gettysburg Address

Context:

Obviously, the Declaration of Independence, with its "all men are created equal" creed, and the nation's practice of slavery were at odds. To live its creed, the nation had to abolish slavery. As mentioned previously, Jefferson feared that, allowed to continue, slavery would surely wreck the new nation. Though a slave owner himself, he advocated its abolition, but thought its successful abolition depended on a democratic process in which slave owners consented to free their slaves in a wide-scale emancipation act. This, of course, did not happen. The issue became more and more heated as abolitionists pushed harder and harder for abolishing slavery while supporters pushed to expand it into new states and territories. Finally, as we have previously stated, the issue divided the states into the North and the South—the North, called the Union, opposing slavery and the South, called the Confederacy, defending slavery. The Civil War began in April of 1861 when Confederate soldiers fired on Union-held Fort Sumter, South Carolina, and it effectively ended at the battle of Appomattox, Virginia, in April of 1865, the Union winning. Thus, the fourth stop of our historical tour will focus on President Abraham Lincoln's judicious leadership in managing to officially abolish slavery without permanently splitting the nation. Lincoln's judicious leadership is, no doubt, characterized in the following anecdote. When an elderly resident of the Union North asked President Lincoln why he did not destroy his Southern enemies, he answered, "Madam, do I not destroy my enemies when I make them my friends?"

Is Lincoln not implying the best way to destroy an enemy is to make him your friend, and that is the way he is attempting to deal with his Southern enemies? Surely so.

Looking beyond this anecdote, two famous historical events, the Emancipation Proclamation (1863) and the Gettysburg Address (1863),[14] furnish undeniable evidence of Lincoln's judicious leadership. In the Emancipation Proclamation, he states, "That on the first day of January, in the year of our Lord one thousand eight hundred and sixty-three, all persons held as slaves within any State or designated part of a State the people whereof shall then be in rebellion against the United States, shall be then, thenceforward, and forever

---

[14] To view these two documents, see Miller, *Heritage of American Literature*, 1999–2001.

free; and the Executive Government of the United States, including the military and naval authority thereof, will recognize and maintain the freedom of such persons, and will do no act or acts to repress such persons, or any of them, in any efforts they may make for their actual freedom." Thus, the Emancipation Proclamation not only added moral dimension to the Union effort but also enhanced its military strength by freeing thousands of slaves who would be free to join the Union armies.

In tandem with Lincoln's Emancipation Proclamation is his Gettysburg Address, an unforgettable speech that garnered enduring acclaim. The occasion of the speech was the dedication of the National Cemetery at Gettysburg, the site of one of the bloodiest battles of the Civil War and the battle whose Union victory spelled defeat for the Confederacy. The purpose of the speech was to commemorate the occasion. Lincoln, however, was not the featured speaker. That honor was assigned to the renowned orator of that day, Edward Everett, who gave a speech lasting for two hours. President Lincoln followed with his two-minute address, a commemoration in which he addressed the purpose of winning the Civil War: to abolish slavery and to preserve the Union.

Let us carefully note what he said. "Four score and seven years ago our fathers brought forth on this continent a new nation, conceived in liberty, and dedicated to the proposition that all men are created equal." The word *score* adds a biblical touch (King James translation)[15]; the four score and seven years define the number of years since the Declaration of Independence (1776), the birth of the nation, in which our founding fathers "dedicated to the proposition that all men are created equal." Note that Lincoln is calling attention to the statement in the Declaration of Independence that we've been referring to as the nation's creed—"We hold these truths to be self-evident, that all men are created equal, that they are endowed by their Creator with certain inalienable rights, that among these are life, liberty, and the pursuit of happiness; that to secure these rights, governments are instituted among men, deriving their just powers from the consent of the governed.'" Lincoln continues, noting that now, eighty-seven years later, the nation is engaged in a great civil war testing that proposition, that exemplary creed our founders envisioned and declared. "We have come," continues Lincoln, "to dedicate a portion of that field [the National Cemetery], as a final resting place for those who here gave their lives that that nation might live." So that its founders' proposition—the exemplary creed that all men are created equal—can long endure. "But, in a larger sense," he continues, "we cannot dedicate—we cannot consecrate—we cannot hallow this ground…It is for us the living, rather, to be here dedicated to the unfinished work which they who fought here have thus far so nobly advanced. It is rather for us to be here dedicated to the great task remaining before us—that from these honored dead we take increased devotion to that cause

---

[15] Since Lincoln was an avid reader of the Bible—the King James version, the most-read version of his day—the word *score* (meaning twenty years) would be readily associated with the Bible from the much-referenced Psalm 90:10: "The days of our years are threescore years and ten; and if by reason of strength they be fourscore years."

for which they gave the last full measure of devotion—that we here highly resolve that these dead shall not have died in vain—that this nation, under God, shall have a new birth of freedom—and that government of the people, by the people, for the people, shall not perish from the earth."

TOUR GUIDE REFLECTS ON STOP FOUR

Thus, Lincoln, eloquently and passionately, communicates three major points: "that those dead shall not have died in vain—that this nation, under God, shall have a new birth of freedom—and that government of the people, by the people, for the people, shall not perish from this earth."

Is there doubt that this great address nudged the nation forward in its pursuit of the exemplary? Certainly not in the mind of Edward Everett, the great orator of the day and featured speaker at the occasion. He later wrote Lincoln saying, "I should be glad, if I could flatter myself that I came as near to the central idea of the occasion, in two hours, as you did in two minutes."[16] Everett readily recognized the extraordinary ability of Lincoln to communicate the essence of America's existence and thereby judiciously guide the nation forward despite internal conflict that had erupted into a civil war.

Has history not recognized the speech as one of the greatest ever? If my own school experience is typical, innumerable older adults can remember having to memorize the Gettysburg Address. It's hardly a stretch to assume that the moral prompting resonating

---

[16] *See Miller, *Heritage of America Literature*, 2000.

from the Emancipation Proclamation and the Gettysburg Address nudged the passage of three new constitutional amendments. Between the years 1863 and 1870, the Thirteenth, Fourteenth, and Fifteenth Amendments were added to the Constitution; the Thirteenth freed the slaves, the Fourteenth made them citizens, and the Fifteenth extended them voting rights.

Although these three constitutional amendments were officially giant steps forward, the reality of their embodiment unfortunately required decades of nudging by wise and judicious leaders. And premier among those leaders is Martin Luther King Jr., whose "I Have a Dream" speech is the subject of our next historical stop.

LET THE TOUR CONTINUE

Please listen carefully as I relate relevant information defining the historical context of our fifth stop.

FIFTH STOP

Time: 1963
Nudger: Martin Luther King Jr.
Event: his speech entitled "I Have a Dream"

Context:

This stop being the fifth stop of our historical tour, perhaps it would be helpful to briefly summarize notable insights revealed by our previous stops. Especially so, since King makes several references to events addressed in those stops.

At our first stop, we noted the exemplary covenant-based "city upon a hill" vision for America that was voiced and its pursuit initiated by the two early Puritan colonies—the Plymouth Colony (1620) and the Massachusetts Bay Colony (1630). At our second stop, we noted all thirteen colonies officially ratifying the exemplary "city upon a hill" vision in their Declaration of Independence. This defining document, adopted by the Continental Congress in 1776, states that in compliance with "the laws of nature and of nature's God," the thirteen colonies declare their right to become a "separate and equal station"—meaning a new nation—and in doing so take on not only an obligation to pursue an exemplary "city upon a hill" vision but also to define and publish to the world that vision in a stated creed: "We hold these truths to be self-evident: that all men are created equal; that they are endowed by their Creator with certain inalienable rights; that among these are life, liberty, and the pursuit of happiness; that to secure these rights, governments are instituted among men, deriving their just powers from the consent of the governed."

As our historical tour reveals, American history, from early in its colonial beginning, has been a pursuit of the exemplary—"a city upon a hill." Despite times of hardened resistance, there have always been judicious leaders to step up and nudge the pursuit forward. Such is noted in our third stop. In the spirit of the 1776 Declaration of Independence, Elizabeth Cady Stanton organized the first women's rights convention in America, a convention which met in Seneca Falls, New York, in 1848, and out of which came the Declaration of Sentiments, a document strongly advocating and judicially justifying equal rights for women. In so doing, Stanton initiated a movement that nudged forward equality for women, perhaps most notable being the addition of the Nineteenth Amendment to the Constitution, giving women the right to vote.

The most glaring stain on America's exemplary vision was slavery, the enslavement of African Americans. Though a slave owner himself, Jefferson—writer of the Declaration of Independence—declared slavery a "moral depravity." True to his conscience, he condemned its practice in an early version of the Declaration; however, the antislavery portion was removed by the Continental Congress in order to obtain approval of the Declaration. At the time, about one-fifth of the population were slaves and about one-third of the declaration's signers—Continental Congress representatives—were slave owners. It was left to the new nation's diehard abolitionists, the Civil War, and Abraham Lincoln's judicious leadership to nudge the pursuit of the exemplary forward by fomenting the moral leverage necessary for the approval of the Thirteenth, Fourteenth, and Fifteenth Amendments to the Constitution.

However, these constitutional amendments, though officially freeing the slaves and making them citizens, did not in reality afford them equality. This miscarriage of justice is the subject of the famous speech—"I Have A Dream"—delivered by Martin Luther King, Jr. in 1963, one hundred years after Lincoln's Emancipation Proclamation. As we have observed, America's pursuit of the exemplary sometimes seemed hopelessly stalled, but at those times, judicious leaders stepped up and nudged the pursuit forward. Again, such is the subject of our fifth stop.

Unquestionably, Martin Luther King, Jr. was an exceptional voice in promoting the Civil Rights Movement of the twentieth century. As Lincoln previously stepped forward to address the issue dividing the nation, the African American slavery issue, so King stepped forward a hundred years later to address the kindred issue still dividing the nation—the continued denial of equal civil rights to African Americans despite passage of the Thirteenth, Fourteenth, and Fifteenth Amendments to the Constitution. King embraces the exemplary "city upon a hill" vision for America initially voiced by Winthrop and codified in the Declaration of Independence, but he judiciously and passionately makes the case that to deny African Americans equal opportunity regarding their civil rights as codified in the Declaration of Independence and ratified in the Constitution is a tragic miscarriage of justice and a gross violation of America's "city upon a hill" vision—which he equates with the American dream.

As references to God and the Bible reveal, King's speech, like Winthrop's sermon, presumes America established to be a divinely enlightened commonwealth, a "city upon a hill" (Matthew 5:14). Yet he passionately makes the case this will never be reality as long as its African American citizens are denied their inalienable rights. This can only be reality, he declares, "when all of God's children will be able to sing with new meaning, 'my country 'tis of thee; sweet land of liberty; of thee I sing.'" King's speech implies that the moral measurement for a "city upon a hill" status requires embodiment of the two commandments declared the greatest: "First, love God with all your heart, soul, and mind. Second, love your neighbor as yourself" (Matthew 22:35–40). King's dream is the American dream as first notably voiced by Winthrop—"we shall be as a city upon a hill"—and restated by Jefferson and ratified by the Continental Congress—"We hold these truths to be self-evident, that all men are created equal." Possessing historical insight, King recognized that the embodiment of this exemplary dream was a challenging process and that, at times, the pursuit of its embodiment required passionate and judicious leadership to nudge it forward.

As Stanton recognized the iconic Jefferson and utilized his rhetorical skills to advance equal rights for women, so King utilized the iconic Lincoln to advance the pursuit of civil rights for African Americans. Standing in front of the Lincoln Memorial in August 1963, one hundred years after Lincoln issued the Emancipation Proclamation (1863) and delivered the Gettysburg Address (also, 1863), King, a student of history, a minister of the Lord, and a master of rhetoric, delivered his historic speech that captivated America. The occasion was the 1963 march on Washington, whereby an estimated 250,000 participants symbolically gathered at the Lincoln Memorial to celebrate the advocacy of civil rights for African Americans. King, sustained by faith, enlightened by historical knowledge, and empowered by rhetorical skill, delivered a speech that penetrated the heart and soul of America. For not only did he address the estimated 250,000 persons facing him at the scene, but he also addressed millions more across the nation facing him on their TV screens. The speech was like a moral mirror held facing the nation and emitting powerful images that penetrated prejudice-sealed minds and softened stony hearts. In the tradition of the founders of America, this latter-day prophet, preacher, and rhetorician sought to expedite the full embodiment of the exemplary "city upon a hill"—call it *vision*, *creed*, or *dream*.

King, as noted, chose to call it *dream*, and used the "I have a dream" refrain throughout the speech to empower his message, which may be stated as follows: *For America to be truly a city upon a hill, its African American citizens must be accorded the same liberties and privileges as its other citizens. All of the nation's citizens must have equal access to the pursuit of happiness as promised in the Declaration of Independence and ratified in the Constitution. All men and women being created in the image of God,*[17] *there is no justification for denying African Americans equality.* Yet a truth lamely stated carries little force regardless of its profoundness. As Marshall McLuhan so aptly communicated in his famous hyperbole, "the medium is the message"—meaning the force of the message depends heavily on its presentation—a lame presentation weakens the force of a profound message! All literary classics exemplify profundity of theme (message) and perfection of technique (medium). Such is the case with King's "I Have a Dream" speech. It ranks in the top category of classic speeches such as Pericles's Funeral Oration and Lincoln's Gettysburg Address, each a speech commemorating a nation's exemplary deeds.

To more fully appreciate the effectiveness of King's classic speech,[18] let's note specific instances in which perfection of technique (medium) clearly enhances profundity of theme (message).

In the first line of his speech, he unmistakably connects with Lincoln *rhetorically* ("five score years ago"), *historically* (1863–1963), and *morally* (the Emancipation Proclamation), thereby connecting his advocacy of African American rights to Lincoln's advocacy thereof a century previous. The Lincoln connection established, King amplifies their just cause by identifying the Emancipation Proclamation (1863) "as a great beacon light of hope to millions of Negro slaves who had been seared in the flames of withering injustice." They perceived this "beacon light of hope…a joyous daybreak to end the long night of their captivity." This dramatic figurative

---

[17] "So God created man in His own image; in His own image He created him; male and female He created them" (Genesis 1:27).

[18] To view *I Have a Dream,* see William Safire, ed., *Lend Me Your Ears: Great Speeches in History* (W. W. Norton & Company, 1997), 333–336.

phrasing of the event unquestionably enhances sympathy for the deserving African American. Continuing in rhetorical mode, he says "one hundred years later the Negro is still languishing in the corners of American society, an exile in his own land." Note that in the first line of his speech, King uses "five score years ago" in order to rhetorically connect to the first line of Lincoln's Gettysburg Address: "four score and seven years ago." Then note that after his first-line connection with Lincoln through the "five score years" phrase, he next uses the equivalent "one hundred years" phrase to emphasize the extensive passage of time. Compare, connotatively, the "one hundred years" phrase to the "five score years" phrase. Though each phrase addresses the same length of time, does not the "one hundred years" phrase greatly magnify, connotatively, the extensiveness of the period of time (1863–1963) that civil rights had been unjustly denied African Americans? Emphasizing this tragic fact, of course, magnifies sympathy for the deserving African Americans. Furthermore, it magnifies the legitimacy of his dream, a dream of furthering the fulfillment of America's foundational dream—a divinely enlightened commonwealth, "a city upon a hill."

As the aforementioned William Bradford might have phrased it, "Here is to be noted a special providence of God." On August 28, 1963, Martin Luther King Jr., a minister of God, a student of history, and a master of rhetoric, delivered the captivating speech that judiciously tweaked America's conscience concerning civil rights, thereby nudging forward the nation's pursuit of the exemplary. Through masterful rhetoric, King validated his case: equal civil rights for African Americans. Referencing time and place,[19] he says,

---

[19] Time: August, 1963; Place: Lincoln Memorial, Washington, DC.

"We have…come to this hallowed spot to remind America of the fierce urgency of *now*." Referencing founder promises, he says, "*Now* is the time to make real the promises of democracy." Referencing faith, he says, "*Now* is the time to open the doors of opportunity to all of God's children." Echoing the social justice prophet Amos, he answers those who ask when African Americans will be satisfied: "We will not be satisfied until justice rolls down like water and righteousness like a mighty stream" (Amos 5:24). Again referencing his faith, he says, "in spite of the difficulties and frustrations of the moment, I still have a dream. It is a dream deeply rooted in the American dream." And to validate his dream, he references the Declaration of Independence, saying, "I have a dream that one day this nation will rise up and live out the true meaning of its creed: 'We hold these truths to be self-evident: that all men are created equal.'" Continuing, he says, "This will be the day when all of God's children will be able to sing with new meaning, 'My country 'tis of thee, sweet land of liberty, of thee I sing. Land where my fathers died, land of the pilgrim's pride, from every mountainside, let freedom ring.' And if America is to be a great nation," he adds, "this must become true."

No doubt, the momentum generated by the 1963 peaceful march on Washington and King's captivating mirror speech provided the needed nudge to move forward the nation's pursuit of the exemplary. Why so? The next year, the United States Congress passed the sweeping Civil Rights Act of 1964, addressing discrimination on the basis of race, color, religion, sex, or national origin.

But in praising King, let us not forget to acknowledge two more leaders who added strength to the "needed nudge" furnished by King—Presidents John Kennedy and Lyndon Johnson. Previous to King's August 8, 1963, speech, Kennedy, on February 28, 1963, addressed congress urging civil rights legislation. To paraphrase, he noted that the Constitution is color blind and that it neither knows nor tolerates classes among its citizens; however, he continues, the country has not conformed to the principles of the Constitution, and having not done so, has left the nation compromised legally and morally. The civil rights issue is not only a constitutional issue; it is a moral issue as well. Thus, the import of Kennedy's message: to examine how far we have come in achieving first-class citizenship for all citizens regardless of color, how far we yet have to go, and what further tasks need to be carried out by the executive and legislative branches of the federal government, the state and local governments, and private citizens and organizations.

Then on June 19, 1963, Kennedy submitted to congress the Civil Rights Act of 1963. Though he was not able to get the proposed legislation passed, Lyndon B. Johnson, the succeeding president, continued the push for its passage, and with the nudge fomented by King's August 28, 1963, "I Have A Dream" speech, an encompassing Civil Rights Act became reality. On July 2, 1964, the Civil Rights Act was passed and signed into law. The American dream of inalienable equal rights took a significant step forward, which is to say, America's "pursuit of the exemplary" took another significant step forward. And again let us note that it happened when inspired leaders, like the founders of this great nation, believed in God and sought to honor the two greatest of his commandments: "Love the Lord your God with all your heart, with all your soul, with all your mind" and "Love your neighbor as yourself" (Matthew 22:35–40).

As Winthrop notes in his sermon, "A Model of Christian Charity," humanity is diverse—rich and poor, weak and strong, eminent and lowly—but ideally bonded through Christian love, the bond of perfection. And as noted throughout this historical tour, the major forward nudges of America's pursuit of the exemplary happen when the *nudger* is a believer, one who believes in God the Creator and that humanity is subject to his will as explicitedly stated in Proverbs 19:21. "Many are the plans in a person's heart, but it is the Lord's purpose that prevails." Thereby, America's context reveals that, when the nation exhibits obedience to the covenant relationship inherent in its foundational vision, it moves forward in pursuit of the exemplary. So as Winthrop advised, let us maintain our obedience by following the counsel of the prophet Micah, who said, "What does the Lord require of you, but to do justly, to love mercy, and to walk humbly with your God?" (Micah 6:8).

Now, with our previous historical tour stops fresh in our minds, let's briefly review the time period between the passage of the 1964 Civil Rights Act and the year 2023, a year in which America notably experiences a national identity crisis. In doing so, we will focus on President Ronald Reagan and President George H. W. Bush.

LET THE TOUR
CONTINUE

SIXTH STOP

Time: 1981

Nudger: President Ronald Reagan

Event: Restoration of that "shining city upon a hill"

Context:

The 1964 Civil Rights Act was followed by the 1965 Voting Rights Act, one intended to eliminate legal barriers at the state and local levels that allowed racial discrimination practices. Next came the 1968 Fair Housing Act prohibiting discrimination involving the sale, rental, or financing of housing based on race, national origin, and gender. Thus, by the end of the 1960s, the Civil Rights Movement had made significant progress in removing racial discrimination as a barrier to "the pursuit of happiness." No longer could persons be denied access to public facilities—restaurants, hotels, transportation, schools—because of the color of their skin or ethnicity. Yet despite the significant civil rights progress that nudged America's pursuit of the exemplary forward, the adverse effects of the prolonged Vietnam War (1955–1975) drained away time, energy, and support from the pursuit.

Reagan began his presidency in 1981 faced with an inflation-ridden economy and America viewed as a failure by other nations, but eight years later in his farewell address, it is a different America. Significant restoration has taken place—restoration largely the result of his leadership.

In his 1989 farewell address[20], Reagan says, "they called it the Reagan Revolution, and I'll accept that, *but for me it always seemed more like the Great Rediscovery: a rediscovery of our* values *and our common sense.*" He goes on to say, "*Common sense* told us that when you put a big tax on something, the people will produce less of it. So, we cut the people's taxes and the people produced more than ever before." Continuing, he says, "*common sense* told us that to preserve the peace we'd have to become strong again after years of weakness and confusion. So, we rebuilt our defenses, and this New Year we toasted the new peacefulness around the globe."

In short, he is saying that a *commonsense* application of our rediscovered *values* brought about the longest peacetime expansion in our history, thereby enhancing family income and reducing poverty. Entrepreneurship is booming, research and new technology are thriving, and America is exporting more than ever before. Thus, a rediscovery of our *values_*and the exercise of *common sense* restored America's role as that "shining city upon a hill" and—let us add to

---

[20] To view Reagan's 1989 farewell address, see *Inaugural Addresses of the Presidents of the United States of America: From George Washington to Joseph R. Biden, Authorized American Patriot Edition, Blue Edge Publishing Group, 2021.*

Reagan's assessment—nudged America forward in its pursuit of the exemplary.

Summing up the lesson learned, Reagan says, *"If we ever forget that we're one nation under God, then we will be a nation gone under."* In this prayerful exhortation, Reagan not only confirms his belief that America was founded to be a city upon a hill, a city (a commonwealth) in a covenant relationship with God as explained by Winthrop in his sermon, "A Model of Christian Charity," but also that the restoration of America that took place during his presidency (1981–1989) was the result of his acting on that belief. Furthermore, this prayer and his frequent citing of the laudatory phrase "a city upon a hill"—which he loved to embellish by adding the word *shining*—that "shining city upon a hill"—presumably expresses his hope that it defines his legacy as an exemplary legacy for future American leaders to follow and future American citizens to discover and to embrace.

LET THE TOUR CONTINUE

SEVENTH STOP

Time: 1989

Nudger: President George H. W. Bush

Event: Spiritual restoration—"a thousand points of light"

Context:

Like Reagan, George H. W. Bush recognized America's role as "a city upon a hill." In his 1989 inaugural address,[21] he thanked Reagan for his outstanding leadership, the kind of leadership that recognized and revered America's "city upon a hill" vision adopted by its founders. Bush is awed and elated to have repeated the same oath of office word for word as George Washington, America's first president, and to have placed his hand on the same Bible on which Washington placed his. Then he says, "My first act as president is a

---

[21] To view George H. W. Bush's 1989 inaugural address, see *Inaugural Addresses of Presidents of the United States: From George Washington to Joseph R. Biden., Authorized American Patriot Edition, Blue Edge Publishing Group. 2021.*

prayer." And requesting heads bowed, he prays, "Heavenly Father, we bow our heads and thank You for Your love. Accept our thanks for the peace that yields this day and the shared faith that makes its continuance likely. Make us strong to do Your work, willing to hear and heed Your will, and write on our hearts these words: 'Use power to help people.' For we are given power not to advance our own purposes, nor make a great show in the world, nor a name. There is but one just use of power, and it is to help people. Help us remember it, Lord. Amen."

As his prayer reveals, Bush recognized the importance of involving every person in the nation in the pursuit of the exemplary. After his prayer, Bush continues, saying "*I have spoken of a Thousand Points of Light*, of all the community organizations that are spread like stars throughout the Nation, doing good. We will work on this in the White House, and in the Cabinet agencies. I will go to the people and the programs that are the brighter points of light, and I will ask every member of my government to become involved. *The old ideas are new again because they are not old; they are timeless: duty, sacrifice, commitment and a patriotism that finds its expression in taking part and pitching in.*" Bush is, and rightfully so, stressing the importance of the exercise of patriotism by all the nation's citizens. As president Kennedy so memorably expressed it, "Ask not what your country can do for you; ask what you can do for your country."

EIGHTH STOP

Time: The Present

Nudger: Hopefully, the People of America

Event: Personal responsibility

Context:

The Hopeful Revelation: Hopefully, the previous seven stops of this historical tour have defined America's foundational vision—"a city upon a hill"—and the pursuit thereof. Hopefully, the tour has revealed that we, the present people of America, in order to continue forming a more perfect nation, need to "pitch in" and do our part in revitalizing our exemplary foundational vision. Hopefully, dear reader, when viewing America's present role in light of our foundational "city upon a hill" vision, you perceive a critical need for a renewed devotion to our foundational vision and thereby feel compelled to assume a *nudger* role, at some attainable level, in facilitating its renewal. Does common sense not tell us that when a nation lacks a commonly shared exemplary vision, the exemplary is not likely to happen? Is it not self-evident that since America is a democracy, we the people are responsible for the role of our nation? Let's listen again to the memorable exhortations on the topic quoted above, the memorable exhortations voiced by President Kennedy and President Bush concerning the people's responsibility. *"Ask not what your country can do for you; ask what you can do for your country,"* voiced by Kennedy. Fulfilling this responsibility requires *"duty, sacrifice, commitment and a patriotism that finds its expression in taking part and pitching in,"* voiced by Bush. Let us, the present people of America, take heed of this sage counsel and, in doing so, pray that recognition and celebration of America's foundational vision spreads, "like a thousand points of light," to every community throughout this nation.

The Hopeful Application: Since pursuit of the exemplary requires a guiding vision, the present people of America, in order to continue forming a more perfect union, have need to be aware of our founders' vision. They need to know what we have witnessed on this historical tour: that our nation was founded on the vision of an exemplary commonwealth, that its vision was expressed in a biblical allusion—"a city upon a hill"—and spelled out in a succinct creed. Although we quoted the creed earlier, let us, for the purpose of memory enhancement, repeat it here. "We hold these truths to be self-evident: that all men are created equal; that they are endowed by their Creator with certain inalienable rights; that among these are life, liberty, and the pursuit of happiness. That to secure these rights, governments are instituted among men, deriving their just powers from the consent of the governed." To the person familiar with America's context, mere reference to the "city upon a hill" allusion or the succinctly stated creed would elicit in the person's mind the exemplary vision embodied therein. Consequently, if we want a common sharing of patriotic feeling toward America, would common sense not tell us—for the purposes of linking the present generation patriotically with the founding generation in a commonly shared, understood, and appreciated relationship—to include in our public educational institutions—our schools, our colleges, our universities—studies portraying the portion of America's context that reveals the nation's founding vision of "a city upon a hill," dedicated to pursuit of the exemplary? And would not such studies generate enlightened patriotic feeling to be commonly shared and thereby enhance commitment to pursuit of the exemplary as envisioned by America's judicious founders? Surely so.

Personal Participation: Individuals can, at the least, participate in promoting exemplary patriotism in their immediate communities. Consider the impact of countless community groups, like "a thousand points of light," focused on prioritizing the nation's foundational vision. Think of the positive impact of the exercise of common sense in promoting the nation's foundational priority—to be that "city upon a hill." Does common sense not tell us that principles ordained by God, the creator, are priority principles? Does common sense not tell us that our nation's creed in compliance "with the laws of nature and of nature's God"—as stated in the Declaration of Independence—is of high priority in pursuit of the exemplary? And does common sense not tell us that historical awareness is essential in preserving and promoting that pursuit? Surely so.

Now that we have the vision and the creed fixed in our own mind, let's think how we, as individuals, might be able to *pass it on*. How can we pass on America's foundational vision of a nation divinely sanctioned to pursue the exemplary principle of equality and inalienable rights? Please consider the following. suggestions.

PASS IT ON **SUGGESTIONS**

*T*o initiate discussion of the topic, ask friends and acquaintances if they are familiar with the phrase "city upon a hill." Likely, responses would be something like—"of course," "maybe," or "don't think so." To any one of these three likely responses, consider utilizing one of the following three suggestions for your *pass it on* responses.

1. If time permits and you feel comfortable doing so, give them a brief summary of *America In Context: A Pursuit of the Exemplary*.

2. If time is limited or you feel disinclined to summarize, suggest they purchase a copy of *America In Context: A Pursuit of the Exemplary*. It is readily available on Amazon.com in paperback or e-book.

3. If you prefer a more novel *pass it on* approach, the resource for implementing it is likely in your wallet or your money clip. Think of the ubiquitous dollar bill. Nowhere is

America's foundational vision and creed more masterfully celebrated than the graphic display on the back of the ubiquitous dollar bill—a bill seen and handled by millions of Americans each day. Yes, the back of the dollar bill documents, through a combination of symbolic imagery and defining statement, the exemplary vision of America's founders and their passionate belief in its divine sanction. How so?

Demonstration Scenario

With a dollar bill and a magnifying glass in hand, seat yourself at a table, desk, or other flat surface, and place the dollar bill face down on it. Now, focusing on this backside of the bill, note that horizontally centered are the words **IN GOD WE TRUST.** Then note the image of the Great Seal of the United States, obverse and reverse (front and back), centered vertically, the obverse on the right side and the reverse on the left.

Next, note on the reverse side the image of the Eye of Providence positioned above an unfinished pyramid of thirteen layers capped by the Latin phrase *Annuit Coeptis,* a motto explaining the symbolism of the eye image. Translated, it reads "He [God] approves our undertakings," and *undertakings* means the thirteen colonies that become the first thirteen states forming the United States of America, hereby represented by the thirteen layers of the unfinished pyramid, an ancient symbol of strength and permanence. Now, again note above the unfinished pyramid the Eye of Providence, a symbol of divine approval and guidance. Next, focus on the bottom layer of the pyramid, and there note the new nation's founding date inscribed in Roman numerals, MDCCLXXVI—1776. Next, note beneath the pyramid the Latin phrase *Novus Ordo Seclorum*, meaning, "A New Order of the Ages."—this *new order*, of course, being the founding of the exemplary United States of America.

Now, let's note on the obverse side of the Great Seal the image of the bald eagle fronted by the shield of the United States of America. Notice the shield has thirteen red and white stripes representing the thirteen original colonies that became the thirteen original states of the United States of America. Complimenting this achievement, the eagle holds in its beak a banner inscribed with the Latin phrase *E pluribus unum*, meaning "out of many one." Furthermore, the eagle holds an olive branch in the right talon, suggesting a preference for peace, but holds a bundle of arrows in the left talon, suggesting readiness and strength for battle if necessary. Centered above the head of the eagle is a constellation of thirteen stars indicating a blessed new nation taking its place among the sovereign nations of the world. It should be noted that creating the symbolic Great Seal was a high priority for our nation's founders. The Continental Congress began planning a seal only hours after the signing of the Declaration of Independence in 1776. The planning, however, continued through three committees and six years of debate and revision before the final design was approved by Congress in 1782.

Would it not be a great boon to America's pursuit of the exemplary if every resident recognized and understood the following: first, that the Great Seal of the United States documents the "city upon a hill" *vision* of the nation's founders, and second, that through the utilization of the obverse and reverse (front and back) of the

Great Seal, the celebrated vision is inscribed on the back of the ubiquitous dollar bill?

Would not such recognition and understanding serve an exemplary level of good, the good of the individual, the good of the nation, the good of the world? Does Winthrop's sermon "A Model of Christian Charity," not envision an exalted, exemplary level of good? Does the Declaration of Independence, penned by Jefferson—"We hold these truths to be self-evident"—not envision an exalted, exemplary level of good? Does the Stanton addendum—the Declaration of Sentiments declaring that "all men_*and women*_are created equal"—not envision an exalted, exemplary level of good? Does Lincoln's Emancipation Proclamation, followed by his Address, declaring "a government of the people, by the people, for the people"—not envision an exemplary level of good? Does not King's "I Have a Dream" speech declaring the imperative that "all of God's children [must] be able to sing with new meaning: 'My country 'tis of thee, sweet land of liberty'"—represent an exemplary level of good? Did Reagan's reverence for and celebration of "that shining city upon a hill" vision not inspire an exemplary level of good? Likewise, was Bush's vision of a "thousand points of light" not a *city upon a hill* vision and thereby an exemplary level of good? Is President Kennedy's memorable exhortation, "Ask not what your country can do for you; ask what you can do for your country" not a *city upon the hill* concept and thereby an exemplary level of good? In summary, does common sense not tell us, "America, embrace your founders' *city upon a hill* vision; America, resume your pursuit of the exemplary"?

Historically, is it not when our elected leaders recognize, revere, and pursue our founders' exemplary vision that America's pursuit of the exemplary prevails? For example, witness the Reagan era. President Reagan enthusiastically reminded America of its role as that "city upon a hill," often adding the complimentary prefatory word "shining"—that "shining city upon a hill." Likewise, is it not instructive that when our elected leaders fail to recognize, revere, and pursue our founders' exemplary vision, that our nation's pursuit of the exemplary falters? For example, witness the present stalemate[22] of America's pursuit of the exemplary.

But let us not despair. Hopefully, we the people of this great democracy, America, will exercise our civic duty and come to the aid of our country by lending a commonsense ear to the candidates whose names will be appearing on our ballot and thereby be prepared to mark that ballot judiciously. To do so, it is imperative to lend an attentive ear to each candidate in our jurisdiction on the elective pyramid—local, state, and national. And on the fourth year, lend an especially attentive ear to each candidate seeking the office at the very pinnacle of the elective pyramid—the office of the president.

May common sense, like a thousand points of light, awaken in every community of America the importance of America's foundational vision: *"a city upon a hill"*—a commonwealth, a nation, dedicated to *pursuit of the exemplary.*

---

[22] The present of this writing being 2023.

Dear reader, thank you for touring America's context for the purpose of focusing on the nation's foundational vision and the pursuit thereof. Hopefully, presenting the relevant historical event at each stop, as if it were happening while you watched and listened, has created a sense of immediacy between you and the event—and consequently, you, dear reader, are experiencing positive *nudger-mode* vibes—that is to say, *thinking of ways to become personally involved helping nudge America forward in pursuit of the exemplary.*

COMMONSENSE QUESTIONS TO KEEP IN MIND

Should not America place high priority on reviving and maintaining interest in and commitment to our founders' exemplary vision—"a city upon a hill"?

Should not that vision be introduced and explained to all current American residents, to each new generation of native-born Americans, and to each new immigrant to America?

Though there is strength in diversity, should we not have a commonly shared directive to bypass inevitable conflicts that invite chaos?

And should that commonly shared directive not be our foundational vision—"a city upon a hill," America's pursuit of the exemplary?

And America being a democracy, is it not the initiative of its citizens, or lack thereof, which determines whether the nation functions as an exemplary "city upon a hill" or flounders as a confused city on downhill decline?

Dear Reader, My Closing Thought:

*Let us not lose our common sense and thereby
lose our pursuit of the exemplary!*

END OF TOUR

*May God Bless You,
May God Bless America,*

Bob Dowell

WORKS REFERENCED IN THIS TRAVELOGUE

The Bible: References are generally limited to simply the book, chapter and verse, otherwise accompanied by a paraphrase or short quote from the nkjv or niv.

Miller, James E. Jr., ed., *Heritage of American Literature:* Vol. I, *Beginnings to the CivilWar.* Harcourt Brace Jovanovich, 1991.

Inaugural Addresses of the Presidents of the United States of America: From GeorgeWashington to Joseph R Biden, Authorized American Patriot Edition, Blue Ridge Publishing Group. 2021.

Safire, William, ed., *Lend MeYour Ears: Great Speeches in History.* W. W. Norton & Company, 1997.

Sheats, R. A., ed., *The New-England Primer.* Psalms 78 Ministries, 2012.

APPENDIX

Dear Reader,

I am including this appendix to explain my use of the terms *Old World* and *New World* in this historical travelogue. I view the Jewish culture, the Greek culture, and the Roman culture as the supreme cultures of Old World Western Civilization. Concepts embodied in these three cultures were brought to New World America by early colonists. As our historical travelogue reveals, these Old World concepts significantly influenced the development of an exemplary Western Civilization culture in New World America.

Please view the graphic chart below that traces the development and pursuit of the exemplary[23] in Old World Western Civilization. The intent of the chart is to highlight the development of the *supreme noble ideal* embedded in the Old World context and how that ideal, in turn, significantly influenced the development of the exemplary in the New World America context.

---

[23] Please note that I have labeled the pursuit of the exemplary depicted on the chart as the *supreme noble ideal* in Western Civilization.

FURTHER EXPLANATION OF THE CONTEXT CHART BELOW

First, note that I have posted the names of the cultural centers representing the three supreme cultures of the Old World:

> Jerusalem representing the Jewish culture;
> Athens representing the Greek culture;
> Rome representing the Roman culture.

Second, note that under each name center, I have quoted a succinct statement reflecting the supreme noble ideal of that culture.

Third, note that the quote under Jerusalem comes from the Bible, that the quote under Athens comes from the Greek epic, the *Iliad*, and that the quote under Rome comes from the Roman epic, the *Aeneid.*

Then, note that the three cultures meet at the cross: A Hebrew (Jewish) prophet is condemned to death by a Roman governor in a Greek-speaking world. Of course, this so-called prophet proves to be the long-prophesied messiah. Though generally rejected initially as such, his steadfast disciples, utilizing the universal language of Greek and the infinite roadways of Rome, spread Christianity throughout the Roman Empire, and their converts, in turn, spread Christianity throughout the Western world.

Next, note that under Philadelphia, the early cultural center in the New World America, the quote comes from the Declaration of Independence.

The material below is intended to graphically illustrate the origin of,
and the enduring emphasis on,
the supreme Noble Ideal implicit in Western Civilization: emphasis on
Individual Worth (Human Dignity)

------------OLD WORLD------------

Jerusalem
From the Bible: "God created man in His own image; in the image of God He created him;
male and female He created them" (Genesis 1:27).

Athens
From the Iliad: "When many assemble together follow
him who advises best counsel" (IX, 74).

Rome
From the Aeneid: "Remember Roman, to rule the people
under law, to establish the way of
peace, to battle down the haughty,
to spare the meek. Our fine arts,
these, forever" (Book VI).

Three cultures merge at the Cross: A Hebrew prophet is condemned to death by a Roman governor in a Greek speaking world.
Then Jewish believers utilizing the universal language, Greek, and traveling safe Roman roads
spread Christianity throughout the Empire, and their converts throughout the Western world.

------------NEW WORLD------------

Philadelphia
From the Declaration of Independence: "We hold these truths to be self-evident: that all men are created
equal; that they are endowed by their Creator with certain
inalienable rights; that among these are life, liberty and the
pursuit of happiness."

Also by Bob Dowell

Understanding the Bible: Head and Heart
Part One—The Old Testament

Understanding the Bible: Head and Heart
Part Two—Matthew through Acts

Understanding the Bible: Head and Heart
Part Three—Romans through Revelation

Papa, Tell Us About the Bible

Satan and Me and OBE:
An Out of Body Experience

What Makes America Great

Poems About Things That Mattered Most

>>

These books are available in e-book and paperback at
Amazon.com and **BarnesandNoble.com**

>>

Author Bob Dowell, PhD, brings an engaging freshness to his topics through creative utilization of genre:

Poetry in *Understanding the Bible: Head and Heart;*
Drama in *Papa, Tell Us About the Bible;*
Dialogue in *Satan and Me and OBE;* and
Travelogue in *America in Context: A Pursuit of the Exemplary.*

9 798877 530867